Parkinson's,

Poetry,

Art

and Me

Selected Poems and Art by Lynn Martin McHale

Sept 1, 2019

Margaret,
   I hope you find some
inspiration in a poem or
phrase that touches you!

   Lynn McHale

Copyright © 2019 Lynn McHale

Supervising Editor: Irene Zelis

Front cover photography: John C. Spence III

ISBN: 9781092711722

Acknowledgements

Thank you to my family and friends who have loved, supported and encouraged me. You pushed me beyond what I thought I could do. You are all very special to me and I love and thank each of you.

Thank you to Donna Sperlakis, former Coordinator of Movement Disorder Program at Rush Copley Hospital in Aurora, IL., now Director, Community Engagement at Parkinson's Foundation in Chicago area. She is a mix of laughter, smarts, personality, compassion and love, especially for her "group."

Thank you to Melissa Hedlund, founder and Executive Director of The Light of The Heart, a not-for-profit Community Art Therapy Project, for her conviction that art therapy heals. Her support gave me the confidence to create and listen to my soul.

Thank you to Peggy McGahan, art instructor, free-lance artist, and member of Nature's Artist Guild at Morton Arboretum, Lisle IL. I learned so much about watercolor paint and pencil and technique from her. She does beautiful watercolor paintings.

Thank you to Irene Zelis, my new friend for the last 3 years. We discovered we are so much alike, it's scary! She is the first with whom I shared my poems, and through her encouragement, I decided to publish. She thought my poems conveyed important messages and should be shared to benefit others struggling to live with Parkinson's disease. Irene is also the editor.

I want to acknowledge the people I've had the privilege of meeting who have Parkinson's, their care providers, the volunteers at walks, events, fundraisers, my contacts in APDA national office in NY, my board members when I was Board President of APDA Midwest Chapter. Everyone has a story that becomes a part of my Parkinson's journey.

Introduction

Parkinson's, Poetry, Art and Me is the fusion of my poetry and art: photos of my original art, or original photography.

This "fusion" expresses the emotional battle within after I was a diagnosed with Parkinson's disease. I had so many emotions, thoughts, anger and un-answered questions swirling in my head. I started writing, and it came out as poetry.
Initially, I started writing about my anger, emotions and thoughts about having Parkinson's. Overtime as I moved closer to acceptance, I found other subjects to write about; just a word or a random thought or a phrase, or a crazy word rhyme or something I observed would trigger the inspiration for start of my next poem.

Together, my poetry and the creative expression of my art, provide a glimpse into the soul and mind of someone living with Parkinson's disease. Original photography and photos of my original art accompany many of my poems. My hope is that by sharing my work, that maybe some phrase, or image, or poem connects with you or touches something inside you and helps you recognize there is still more to your life living with Parkinson's.

If you look beyond yourself and your situation, there is still the world around you that you may now perceive differently. You can still be an active contributor, there are so many needs in the world. Look for the small pleasures every day and be grateful for each one. If you are really blessed, you are sharing each day with individuals who are positive and lift you up and bring you sunshine with a smile!

My debut book, _Parkinson's, Poetry, Art and Me_ can be purchased on my web site, along with my original framed art and notecards.
Please visit me on Facebook.
Thank you, Lynn McHale

Table of Contents

Chapter One - *I Can't Have Parkinson's* 1

Ambushed 1

Owner's Manual for Walking 2

The ABC's of PD 3

Chemical Warfare 6

Brain Envy 7

Our Menu Has Changed 8

See Me 10

Did Humpty Dumpty Have Parkinson's? 11

Try 12

Worry 13

Just Pretend 14

Just "Lynn" 15

Neuro-Nibbles 17

The Power of I Am…And 19

The "Unknown" is "Really Known" 23

Hot Tea and Cancer 25

The Sound 27

Unnerved 29

Two H's and a J 30

The Soul Box 31

Chapter Two – *That 1 + 1 Thing* 32

Maybe, Someday 32

Just One More Time … Sometime 33

Relationship Roulette 34

The Incomplete Heart 35

Rock Solid 37

Sadder than Sad 38

Ache 39

It's More than Rotating your Tires 40

Right 42

Substance Abuse 44

Indifference Cuts Like a Knife 45

Reveal 47

A Question Posed 49

Chapter Three - *What Comes into My Head* 50

A Cat, a Heart, and Humpty 50

Do You Ever Wonder? 52

The Accident 54

Dream Bubble 55

Curtain Call – Second Act 56

"I'm Sorry," or " I Apologize," or "I was Wrong." Which is it? 59

Misinterpretation 60

Conscious Helplessness 61

Hurt Surfaces 62

Melissa, the Marathon Runner 63

Betty Eyes Her Future 65

Obligation 66

Re-define or Re-design? 67

Medicine Chest...68

Unravel...70

The Pandora Bracelet 73

Chapter Four - *Perfectly Natural*.............................74

Mother Nature is a Terrorist 74

The Storm Dreader...77

Stuck on the Weather Channel....................................79

Finally, Sunshine! 80

Beauty Felled 82

White Weather 83

Soft, Warm Water 84

Je Suis un Artiste 86

My Mosaic Masterpiece 87

Windows 88

Dream Catcher...90

Reflections in a Gazing Ball 92

The Thing About Crystal Balls....................................94

The Spark! To Sparkle!..96

The Path..99

Familiar Roads..100

My Mother's Eyes..101

The Ties That Bind 102

Chapter Five - *Fragmented Feelings* 104

Impermanence..104

Will I Ever See Him Again?..106

New Life...107

Count Every Day..108

Plight...110

Don't Gotta..111

I'm Sorry 112

In the Midst 113

Tonight, It Seems 114

About the Author...115

Chapter One - *I Can't Have Parkinson's*

Ambushed

In my mind,
I am blind
To the fact,
Can't react.

I can walk,
I can talk,
In a certain way,
Brings me such dismay.

Why am I like this?
I'd like to dismiss.
Why are they like that?
Caught, constant combat.

I wage war with transmitters,
Being ambushed is bitter.
My enemy deep within,
 I will never, ever win.

Great funds are being raised,
Enemy not even phased.
To fight the good fight.

There is no flight, no flight!

Owner's Manual for Walking

For most people walking is like breathing; natural,
Don't have to think about it at all,
It's easy, mechanics just seem to work,
Gait is smooth, not with a jerk.

I watch other people walk,
Envious of their grace and stride,
No hesitation, no balk,
No replay tape running inside.

"Bring your leg around, don't drag it,"
"Heel hits first, toes upward,"
"Remember to swing arm, shoulders back,"
"Don't look down, hold head a proper angle."

Think about mechanics of each step,
Concentrate so it all comes together,
Repeat the process again and again,
Need owner's manual for walking.

The ABC's of PD

A   Always with you, Anger, Art therapy, APDA, Art classes, Anonymous grant, Ask for help, Answers, Acceptance!

B   Be the Best you can Be, Balance, BIG, Be Brave, Be happy, Be your own advocate!

C   Caregiver, Contrast, Constipation, Cure, Carries', Christine, Can't be happening!

D   Dopamine, Diagnosis, Delay the Disease, DBS, Disability, Depression, Day to Day, Denial, Donna, Diana, Dave, Dyskinesia, Dystonia, Driving, Deal with it!

E   Evident in Every step, Exercise, Encouragement, Exhausting!

F   Family, Friends, Fun, Fear of Falling, Fatigue, Future, Fine motor skills, Foot problems, Food, Friendship, Fox Trials, Forget this!

G   Gait, Gloom, Get out, Get Going, Get help, Grief, Good Grief!

H   Humor, Handwriting, Hope, Honesty, Home sweet Home, Help!

I   I am ready to work out, Individual, Incontinence, Isolation, I wish I didn't have It!

J   Journey, Jerky muscles, Joint pain, Judy, Just deal with it! Just saying!

K   Kinky muscles, Kindred spirits, Karl, Kiss of death, Kind, Kind'a sucks!

L	Loved ones, Levodopa-Carbidopa, Laughter, LSVT, Lee, Laurie, Let's go!
M	Managing, Medicines, Muscle cramps, Music, Massage, Meditation, Movement Disorder Specialist, Make new friends, Michael J. Fox, Muhammad Ali, Move!
N	Neurologist, Neuro-psychologist, Neuro-ophthalmologist, Neuro-transmitters, NPF, Newsletters, New friends, Not so good, Not fair, Not me!
O	Opportunities, On/Off, Oprah cannot help, Oh ___!
P	Promise of tomorrow, Positive attitude, Personal trainer, Patience, Poetry, Pursuit, Perception, Prescriptions, Peace, Pissed off!
Q	Questioning, Quest for answers and cure, Quiet your mind, Quit – cannot quit!
R	Reeling from diagnosis, Realization, Rigidity, Rut, Rush-Copley Healthplex, Retirement, Recreation, Research, Ready to take charge!
S	Support group, Socialize, Swim, Spirit, Share Story, Slowness, Substantia-Nigra, Stand tall, Susan, Stephanie, Symposiums, Swallowing, Scared, Sucks!

T	Tomorrow, Thankfulness, Today is best day of my life! Tremors, Trying, Trials, Tai Chi, Treadmill, Tired
U	Understanding it all, Until tomorrow, Ugly, Utter devastation!
V	Vision issues, Volunteer, Vulnerable, Voice, Vacation!
W	Why me? What do I do? What's next? Water exercise, Wish for bowel movement, WEB MD, Wishing, Walking, Writing, Wrapping head around it!
X	Exercise, Example, Exactly, Expensive, Exasperation
Y	Yearning for how you were before PD, Yoga, Yes, you have PD, Yikes!
Z	Zealous approach to learning all you can, Zest for living and taking care of yourself, Zen, Zoo –go visit!

Chemical Warfare

Brain battles rage inside my head.
Cells falter, some already dead.
Crucial messages not getting through,
The chemical serving very few.

My brain engages in chemical warfare.
Battles rage over Dopamine, an agonist, rare.
In great demand, only a little bit,
Skirmishes over how much to transmit.

Which cells will occupy the Dopamine?
Never a winner, so cruel, and so mean.
Never a truce, never any R and R,
There are no heroes, it's all very bizarre.

Same battle fought over and over,
Absolutely no end to this war,
Each side losing more and more precious ground,
Cells depleted, no reinforcements found.

Brain Envy

My brain is a neurological time bomb,
It's ticking, but it can't even do that right,
Try so hard, impossible to remain calm,
It's all due to dopamine famine, a blight!

I exercise, play brain games,
Do pretty good, get them mostly right,
Almost feel like I used to, the same,
Many days want to escape, take flight.

Take flight, how? Too anxious to fly.
Escape, where? I'm a prisoner.
Positive thinking, I try, try.
My brain is now a foreigner.

I have brain envy.
I want their brain,
A working brain for me,
Not my drain brain!

I have brain envy,
So, call me selfish,
I want one for me,
A brain I can cherish

Our Menu Has Changed

Let's face it, at some time
We all need to call the doctor's office.
We need to talk to someone;
A nurse, physician assistant, doctor.
We'd settle for any warm body
At the other end of the line.

I'm doing it.
I'm calling the doctor's office,
I have to talk to someone,
I've held off as long as possible,
I hate to be a complainer.

I have questions,
I need answers,
I don't feel good,
My meds aren't working,
My symptoms are worse,
I feel anxious,
I'm having a meltdown,
I just need to complain.

I'm calling!
I'm dialing!
It's ringing!
I'm listening!

Please listen carefully, as our menu has changed, and you are out of options:

Press 1: if you feel you've been f_____ by Parkinson's
Press 2: if the song "shake, rattle, and roll" is stuck in your brain
Press 3: if you are angry and bitter because you have PD
Press 4: if you feel like shit
Press 5: if your medicine is making you nauseous
Press 6: if you are hallucinating
Press 7: if you think you called because you are hallucinating
Press 8: if you feel depressed and apathetic
Press 9   if you don't care that you don't care
Press 10 – if you think you have been misdiagnosed and don't really have PD

Press star if you need these options repeated, oh sorry, we will only say them once.
You should have been listening more closely
You may hang up and end this call at any time
Yes, I think I'll just end it!

See Me

Warm covers, cold morn,
Yet, I am so torn,
I want to leap out of bed,
But something in my brain is dead.

I want to go outside and play,
My option is inside to stay.
I want to run and jump and fly,
But so many days I just cry.

I want the freedom of my youth,
But I must confront the truth.
My strength and agility trapped inside,
I am left with only my pride.

I want to be me, who I used to be.
Now, only this other person you see.
I look at others and wish to be them,
I too want to shine like a brilliant gem.

This person who mourns for who she was before,
If just something, someone to implore.
Doesn't like who she has become,
Now literally walks to beat of a different drum.

Did Humpty Dumpty Have Parkinson's?

Did HD have PD?
Was his balance "off" in the story,
When he sat on the wall, and then fell,
Or just plumpty as we hear tell?

What could the King's men and horses do?
Do you think Humpty should sue?
If he had been given L-dopa
Could he have been fixed up-a?

Try

What's to be positive about?
Let me search deep inside,
Let me find out and shout, and shout.
I have self -worth, dignity, pride.

How far must I travel?
I am tough, I am strong,
Mile after mile, can't unravel.
Inside, I sing my song.

"I am me, I am me,"
"I laugh, I cry,"
"I am sad, I am happy,"
"I can try, I can try!"

I have patience,
I can try.
Even more patience,
Can I try?

I can't win,
I can't show,
I can only place,
Yes, this is a race!

Worry

All my aches and pains,
Whether old or new,
Cause me to exclaim,
Will I end up cold and blue?

Worry about every pain,
Will my cancer return,
How will it come again?
Another illness's turn?

I worry so much,
Seems like all the time,
Is it such and such,
Will I run out of time?

Time is so precious,
Want to be a Grandmother.
Hush sweet baby, hush,
Let me sing you another.

Just Pretend

Some days my mind plays games with me,
It pretends we don't have PD,
Thinks about all the things we can do,
Then, oops, limited to just a few.

Some things I can still do, who knew.
Some things I can't do, know that too.
Oh, so sad and true, makes me blue.

I look at what I see,
Am I picture of PD?
Can't believe this is me.

Just want it to flee,
Just want to be me.
Person I used to be.

Just "Lynn"

Henceforth, and from this day forward,
I am to be known as Lynn.
Not the old Lynn, or regular Lynn,
Not current Lynn, or used to be Lynn,
Just "Lynn!"

I remain the same person, Lynn,
My soul and being define me.
Parkinson's has altered some aspects of me,
But it has not changed the person I grew up to be.

Now for this section
Imagine I listed all the names I've had,
Maiden name, middle name, Confirmation name,
Last names from two marriages.
(All that would be dumb to put on internet).

This is who I am, me!
All the lives lived with these names,
Sum total life of a little girl,
Who grew up to be "Lynn,"
Who happens to have PD!

Neuro-Nibbles

Nasty nibbles in the Nigra,
Bite size bits eaten away.
Neurological Pac Man,
He's here to stay!
He cheats, you say!

Must hold on, delay,
A lesser you, such a crime,
Already lost this game,
Depleted precious time,
No reason, no rhyme.

Neuro-nibbles in the Nigra,
A neurological foray.
A nosh here, a nosh there,
Curse the Nigra I say,
Cure the nibbles, now, today!

My made-up word and definition: Neuro-nibble;
short for neurological nibble. It is what happens in your
brain when you have Parkinson's disease, a degenerative
brain disorder. The brain does not produce enough
dopamine, a chemical needed by neuro-transmitters to
communicate to all parts of the body. Therefore, each and
every day, day after day, tiny neuro-nibbles occur in your
brain as dopamine becomes scarcer. You don't feel the
neuro-nibble, or even sense it is happening. But, over
months, and years the cumulative effect takes its devastating

toll as the brain continues to degenerate, one little neuro-nibble at a time.

The Power of I Am…And

I **am** the soul, spirit and essence of me.
I **am** Lynn, who happens to have PD, a chronic illness,
Not PD patient, who happens to be Lynn.

I have the Power.
I own the Power.
I **am** the Power.

The Power to be independent, **and** to be dependent.
The Power to be separate, **and** to join in.
The Power to participate, a**nd** to take a back seat.
The Power to lead, **and** to follow.
The Power to find my own way, **and** to go with tried
and true.
The Power to explore, **and** to travel the beaten path.

The Power to be Lynn:
Interesting
Funny
Intelligent
Attractive
Caring
Loving
Exhilarating
Physically fit
who happens to have Parkinson's

The Power not to be that poor soul that has Parkinson's,
and who happens to be Lynn!!

I don't have to be one way or the other way exclusively.
I have the freedom to go back **and** forth between,
As life and situations come my way.
It's the **Power of And**!

AND, I have the Power!
You Own the "My"
Have you heard, or said yourself,

"I'm not having one of my better days."
What is a better day?
On scale of worse, good, better, best?

So, is it less than best?
But, it's better than good?
Or is it worse than good?
So, if it's not worse than good,
And it's not good or best,
THEN it's better.

In between good and best,
Is better.
So, you really are having a better day!
And it's better than the alternative.

Remember a simple, been around for a while adage,
"Today is the Best Day in My Life."
Seemingly simple at face value,
Yet deep when dissected.

It doesn't say, "Today is not one of my better days in my life,"
It doesn't say, "Today is a less than best day in my life,"
It doesn't say, "Today is a better than good day in my life,"
It doesn't say, "Today is less than better day in my life,"
It doesn't say, "Today is a worse than good day in my life,"
It says, *"Today is the Best Day in My Life."*

Today, there are things you can do,
Actions you can take,
To make your day good,
Then better, even the **best**!
You are the **MY** called out,

Today is the Best Day in **MY** Life."
You are the MY. You own the MY.

My life, **my** thoughts**, my** mood,
My positive attitude,
My positive self-talk,
My responsibility, **my** prayers,
My interests, **my** activities, **my** exercises,
My happiness, **my** goals,
My dreams, **my** hopes,
My future.

It is never too late,
You are never too young or too old,
Even with an illness,
To dream and hope!

Today is the
BEST DAY
IN MY Life

The "Unknown" is "Really Known"

The "Unknown," a future time and space,
A journey ending in an unknown place.
A start that promises an end,
A passage I dare transcend.

I see early onset to later stages,
Mentally I turn ahead the pages,
I imagine the very worst,
I'm living a life, cursed!

The "Unknown" weighs heavily on me,
Causes me angst, such anxiety,
At times, stifling, oppressive,
Can't stop thinking, obsessive!

Try to mentally prepare,
Read, research, become aware,
Even so, images to conjure,
Mind mines to maneuver, oh torture!
One- way ticket to "Unknown",

Final destination, disabled, alone.
Many stops and starts along the way,
Maybe they'll find a cure, you say?

Desperate for alter passage,
One that gives me an advantage,
Sending out a "may day".
Must get out of my own way!

Hot Tea and Cancer

It's a.m. ten to three,
I'm sitting in bed,
Drinking hot tea,
Currently cancer free.

I don't think about it that much,
New battle with Parkinson's Disease,
Put away, like tea cup in hutch.
Hot tea with honey, please!

Why thinking about cancer tonight?
Friend posted photo "Stupid Cancer,"
Opened the wound, Hope now less bright,
Sipping a cup of memories.

Memories of those who lost their battle,
Fortunate ones who wear label "survivor."
Survivor yes, until day you are not.

Another fight; armed, but still defenseless.
Time is not on your side,
Sorry to disagree, Mick.

Hands on clock pull you inside,
Time passes on. Tick, tick, tick.
It's not time on "life support,
It's your life on "time support."

The Sound

Did you hear it?
The sound, you know.
The sound of the other shoe dropping.

Didn't expect it.
The news, you know.
The news from the doctor disclosing.

What it looks like.
The lumps, you know.
The lumps, you can't feel, but been dreading.

Looks suspicious.
Second time, you know.
Second time, there's no curing.

Recall what he said.
Only treat, you know.
Only treat, second time, there's no curing.

Take it all in.
Process it, you know.
Numb, cry, worry, hope; inside screaming.

Retest. Now wait.
Results, you know.
Breathe, safe this time; dread never ending.

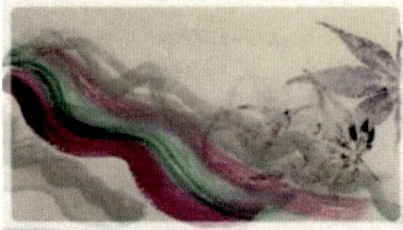

Unnerved

What causes you to be unnerved,
When life's path has curved?
Now, a reason why you swerved,
What purpose has your life served?

Cautious, always reserved,
Reflecting on life observed,
Wanting the best preserved,
Something else delivered.

Insidious, it maneuvered,
Change undeserved,
New reality carved,
Inner workings starved.

Two H's and a J

Can I be happy?
Can I have hope?
Can there be joy?

The Soul Box

Lid wrapped with shiny black trim,
Pink glitter heart,
Ribbons hold it together.

Sides are variations of hand prints,
Colors cascade, intensities interact,
Some are light, optimistic,
Others swirl darker.

A hand reaches out offering help,
Another reaches out asking for help,
There's LYNN in bold pink glitter.
Eyes peeking out amidst curls and feathers,
A scarf partially obscures a soulful glance.

Lift up the lid, reveal her innermost soul,
Peace, solitude, contemplative, beauty,
Truth, creative, expressive, curious,
Dark and light, strong, yet fragile.

A heart at the core, her soul's anchor,
Whispers escape from deep inside,
Listen, learn, live, love your soul.

Chapter Two – *That 1 + 1 Thing*

Maybe, Someday

Maybe… someday… in the future.
Three words; relationship killers.
Steal time, opportunities, happiness,
Steal experiences not lived,
Steal sand from the hour glass,
Steal romances, memories never to be.

Maybe… someday… in the future.
Three words; obvious obstacles.
Never captured smiles in photographs,
Never touched by tenderness,
Never loved, ever lonely,
Never shared lifetime.

Just One More Time … Sometime

To fall in love just one more time,
To feel that knot, such bliss,
To sit and write lines that rhyme,
To anticipate that touch, first kiss.

You anticipate that chance encounter,
You wonder if he's thinking the same,
You wonder if you're empowered,
You don't know how to play this new game.

It's scarier at this point in time,
It's too bad you're not younger, prettier,
It's even worse, you're past your prime,
It's going to be harder, not easier.

After all, you are set in your ways,
After all, you are in decline,
After all, you even got some grays,
After all, is now really sometime?

What is the outcome, what's the answer?
Just give it some time.
What will become of him and her?
Sublime or love crime?

Relationship Roulette

Relationship roulette,
Pull the trigger on one,
Holster the other,
Check the release,
Is it hard to pull,
Or easy to the touch
Half-cocked,
Saturday night special.

Bullets pierce,
Wounding the heart,
Tearing it in pieces,
Edges catch on past lovers' intentions.

Soft target
Bulls eye
Caught in the cross hairs
Sniper
Dead aim
Shoot to kill
Take a gamble
Spin the table
Spin the barrel
Load another clip.

The Incomplete Heart

The Incomplete heart,
Waits still for one dart,
Shot from Cupid's bow,
Love, yet to bestow.

The incomplete heart,
Beats alone … apart.
Bleeds from past arrows,
Passage in … narrows.

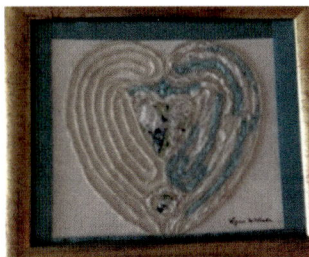

The incomplete heart,
Alone from the start,
What remains, injured,
Love's loss yet endured.

The incomplete heart,
Pierced by that one dart,
A most willing target,
Struck by love or regret.

The incomplete heart,
Longs so for new start,
Essentially empty,
Courts compatibility.

The incomplete heart,
Desires love, an art!
Craves a connection
Anticipation!

The complete heart,
Two halves once apart,
Joined as one, bound now.
It's you, this I vow.

Rock Solid

At one time, I loved you hard.
My love was rock solid.
Precious metals pulsed through my veins,
Filling me with a lustrous, glowing love.

You mined deep within the caverns of my soul.
Picking and shoveling away, one load at a time.
Each load removed left me more and more empty.
Dynamite blasted what "was possible,"
Into rocky bits of what is "now impossible."

Nothing left to pick.
Nothing left to shovel.
Nothing left to unload.
Nothing left, but to shut down.

At one time, I loved you hard.
My love was rock solid.
I once was lustrous and glowed.
My precious metals depleted.
Veins no longer pulsing, collapse.

You held a precious stone in your hand.
You cast it away.
Back into the darkness.
Still lustrous.

Sadder than Sad

Can one be even
Sadder than sad,
When all the plans you
Thought you had
Are just that, plans.
Never to be lived.

 Can one be even
Sadder than sad,
When all the plans you
Thought you had
Are never to happen.

He showed me how things could be,
Then took it all away from me,
Hinted on occasion he'd return,
I can only wait and wait and yearn.

A deep abiding sorrow,
Not enough time,
Not enough tomorrows
Can ever heal it,
Can ever take it away.

Ache

My heart is broken in pieces,
Too many scattered over time.
Old wounds gashed open,
My heart bleeds, cries out!

Tears of agony overflow,
Blur my eyes,
Stream down my face,
Warm salty droplets
Moisten my lips,
Disappear on my tongue,
Follow contour of my jaw,
Pool in that notch at base of neck,
Waiting for a tissue to wipe away the sadness,
Sadness that cannot be wiped away.

My lungs gasp for air,
Between sobs soaked with sorrow.
My soul weeps for what it wants,
For what it may never get.
Time is running out.
My patience is waning.
Am I wasting my time?
Am I squandering my love?

It's More than Rotating your Tires

When did you stop being the daring driver?
Becoming the passive passenger?
Who is driving this relationship?
Who is lugging the baggage,
Stowing it away in trunk for safe keeping?
You want the all-points, major tune-up.
You want more than rotating your tires.

You want "**the works!**"
The all out, everything special deal.
You are the luxury package;
All shiny and bright,
With all the sought- after features.
The perfect make and model.

Individually, all those features can be overwhelming.
Excuses are made for certain features he can live
without.
Already had that once before,
Don't need it again.
That's new, that's different, that's cool!
Picks and chooses what he thinks he wants,
Not sure what he wants or needs.

Taken for a ride, sitting at side of road,
Waiting to be taken home,

Tucked away in safe, dry place.
Want to be kept shiny and bright,
Like new, taken out and shown off.

Want to come screaming over the finish line.
Not as a driver, not as a passenger.
As a team, the pit crew in the relationship race.
Driver and passenger stand together in victory,
Knowing they have run the race, circled the track,
Finished and won as two.

Right

Right place,
Right person,
Wrong time.

Time – past, present, future.
You can't hold on to it.
You can't stop it.
You never have enough.
You have too much.
You don't know how to spend it.
You can't buy it.
You can't give it away.
You can't wish it away.
You can't wish for more.
You can run out.
You can take advantage.

If you meet the right person, in the right place,
Yet the timing is off, what do you do?
Some say, that's just the way it is … Too bad.
One person waits for the other to get to the right time.

If that happens, will they both be at the right time at the
same time?

Do you need to make adjustments to make it the right time? Possibly it's close enough to the right time. Maybe it's just five minutes past the right time or ten minutes before the right time.

It may never be the right time if you are dwelling all the time in the past, and not being present in the present, but hoping for good times in the future.

Substance Abuse

Genuine gestures;
Affirmations of affection,
Simple celebration,
Effortless connection.

Loving expressions of tenderness,
Earnest offerings of concern, access,
Carefree, casual sign of closeness,
Pure, intentional, a gentle caress.

Hollow gestures;
Sincerity feigned, held back,
Plug relationship crack,
Love tepid, open to attack.

Emotional divide wider than a mile,
Insincerities softly spoken with a smile,
Seasoned, served up for quite a while,
Opportunities to beguile.

Empty gestures;
Lacking substance, purposely made,
One is desperate for authenticity,
One is engaged in substance abuse.

Indifference Cuts Like a Knife

Indifference cuts like the blade of serrated knife.
Each time, the jagged edge drags across your wrist,
Just a little drag at first, barely tearing the skin,
Yet the hurt, pain, cuts, and injuries drag on.
They increase in size and frequency,
Until wrist is covered with bloody, torn pieces of skin.

Can't heal.
Don't know how.
Only know how to bleed red tears.
You hurt.
Don't know how to get it to go away.
Can't heal.
Don't know how to live with the pain.
Becomes a part of daily life,
Your constant companion.

Want to live without the pain.
Pain that dwells so deep within.
Don't know how to reach in and pull it out.
Will it hurt? Cutting it out?
Will it hurt more? Keeping it inside?

It's killing you. You know it. You really know it.
You want to cut it out. You really do.
You need to rid your body of it. You really do.

Need to slice through each layer of pain,
Each cut, each bruise inflicted upon you,
Through their indifference.
Need to surgically and precisely remove each layer.
One layer at a time, pain, hurt, indifference.
Need to go underground, deep within yourself to escape.
Need to go underground, down into the dark places to heal.
Need help … Go ask Alice.

Reveal

At what cost to reveal,
A matter of importance,
A secret to conceal,
Trust, honor, and relevance.

How to judge trustworthiness,
How do you know whom to trust?
How to determine timeliness?
You know you should, really must.

It is said, no return to moments before,
It now lays out there, naked.
You have opened and closed the only door,
Rejected or accepted.

If accepted, was it worth it, why driven?
Can't overlook its existence,
Can't go forward, can't ever be forgiven,
Can't pretend, it carries presence.

If rejected, embarrassment, shame, doubt,
Shadow cast, remorse to bear.
Relationship stalled, reason for an out,
Perhaps will end, beyond repair.

Revealing the past from years of living,
Lives forever entangled, always consequence.

Now judging, questioning, wondering,
Wanting ignorance, longing for innocence.
A decision made not to conceal,

Too many questions, reactions invade.
Damn the reveal, hate how I feel,
You and me, revealed truths pervade.

A friend on the line,
A lover not to be,
Wishing for time,
Living in agony.

A Question Posed

A question posed,
An answer given,
A response risked.
Words reluctantly spoken,
Hang in the air,
Occupy space,
Until they fall,
Fall from the air,
No longer there.

Neither hear them fall.
Is question out there,
Is answer out there,
Did both disappear from the air?

Were these words really exchanged?
How long do words hang?
Until either a response,
Until nothing more spoken,
Until whirlwind of words,
Fill the void in space,
Where your words once hung?

Chapter Three - *What Comes into My Head*

A Cat, a Heart, and Humpty

A cat has nine lives.
Humpty couldn't be put back together again.
How many heart aches,
How many heart breaks,
Can a heart endure?
Until a heart
Just can't put all the pieces
Back together again?

It's torn apart.
It' s in shreds.
It's broken in pieces.
So many pieces.

It aches,
It hurts,
It bleeds,
It hemorrhages.
Agony grasps, grips.
Pain spreads slowly,
Seeps deep into soul.
Shatters the mind.
Brings you to your knees,

In the dark of the night.

Desperate for answers.
It renders you hopeless.
It leaves you alone, lost, lonely.
It leaves you unloved.
It leaves you impenetrable.

Do You Ever Wonder?

I need a purpose for my life,
A reason for where I am,
Here, now, at this time.
I wonder.

What will unfold?
Yet to be discovered,
Like clues in a mystery,
Missing puzzle pieces.

Am I the rookie on a chessboard?
A Knight moving every which way?
Or Queen of Hearts in Wonderland?
Yes, I reign in Wonderland.

Wonder, Wander,
Wanderlust, Wanderer,
Wonder why?
Happy Wanderer.
Who is the Happy Wanderer?

Where does he wander?
Why does he wander?
Why is he happy?

I eat Wonder bread,
Tastes wonderful!

Now it all makes sense.
Wonderful, Just Wonderful!

The Accident

Stillness shattered
By distant, wailing sirens.
Sirens that portend tragedy.
The wailing intensifies.

Bodies battered, metal mangled.
Blood splattered, death dangled.
Lives mattered, now entangled.

Strangers in the morning,
On the way to work.
Now victims, taking detour,
On the road to life.

Dream Bubble

Defining, dark, downward descent.
Crashing into abyss of Truth.
Confrontation cries out.

Time to burst my dream bubble,
The place I dwell in my imagination,
My refuge, my perfect world creation.

Why do we create these fantasies?
Why do we dwell in the bubble?
Why do we do this to ourselves?

Why do we do it – hold on so tight?
Why do we do it – keep up the fight?
Why do we do it - romantic's plight!

Curtain Call – Second Act

No more patience!
For those starring in role of a lifetime,
Featuring themselves in lead role,
But playing role of the victim,
But playing role of the martyr,
Always re-reading script of "their story."

Co-starring are excuses and blame,
By far the easiest roles to play,
Don't even have to rehearse,
You've said these lines a hundred times.
They just fall from your mouth naturally, with such
ease.

We've heard the same old lines, same old excuses,
Same old placing blame elsewhere.
Why would we go see you perform in this play?
Why would we accompany you to after-party?
You don't even show up to your own life's party!

Lights dim!
The play closes, bad reviews!
No applause for you in this role,
Your performance is not what it should be!
Needs more effort on your part.
No one wants to see this play,
Even be around you, the lead.

Still blaming others, still seeing yourself as a victim,
Still holding tightly to your script.

Good News
New play is opening,
"Second Chance, Your Second Act."
New role starring you,
New audience with whom to connect,
New script with positive words, phrases and lines.
"Second Chance" comes around once in a lifetime!

Opening Night!
Curtain goes up.
It's you, starring in the role of your life!
Will you open with same old worn out lines?
Lines we have heard again and again.
Or, will we be surprised to hear new lines?
Lines we have never heard or haven't heard in a very
long time.
Lines that at one time in your life brought down the
house!

You have been rehearsing new lines,
Bravely trying them out, speaking loudly,
Watching reactions on their faces,
Measuring responses, looking for connections,
Hoping for applause and an encore!

You only have "Your Second Act,"
Once curtain falls, that starring role ends!

Rave Reviews!
You brought down the house!
You want Critic's final review to read;
How everyone stood up and cheered,
How you had a passion for life,
How you loved all the activities with which you were
involved,
How you greeted each new day as a new opportunity,
How you kept practicing those lines and movements,
Perfecting them to best of your ability,
How you took on another role, and another, and
another,
Never giving up, even when the roles got tougher and
tougher!

Don't squander the opportunity to star in your life's
role!
You deserve rave reviews!!

"I'm Sorry," or " I Apologize," or "I was Wrong." Which is it?

Saying you are sorry,
Saying you were wrong,
Saying you apologize,
Is there a difference among all three?
Subtle?
Major?
In your face?

Does one save face and pride?
Does saying you are sorry,
Carry more weight and meaning?

Does one leave you more vulnerable?
Is one a cop out,
Does it get you off the hook quicker?
Can one be said with less sincerity?
Is one more final?

Misinterpretation

How do words get misinterpreted?
Meanings partially interrupted?
Taking on a dualistic life,
Leading only to discord, strife.

A kindness offered to an old friend,
Taken the wrong way, while on the mend.
Wish it could be withdrawn,
It's out there, I'm the pawn.

Unsettling, not what I meant,
OMG another text sent.
This has to be addressed,
Need to be brave, honest.

Don't want to hurt an old friend,
An explanation I must send,
I hope it's taken the right way,
It can't linger another day.

Conscious Helplessness

I don't know what to do.
Some friends are in bad places.
I really can't help them.

I want to help, I do.
But, only up to a point,
Don't really know how, or even that I should.

It's not that I don't care, I do.
But I can't solve their problems.
Only they can!

Watching as things unravel is difficult,
Listening to struggles they face.
Drowning in their pool of problems.

Limitations exist.
Boundaries are set.
Walls go up.

Handling it poorly,
Distancing myself,
Paying an emotional toll.

Hurt Surfaces

Hurt remembered.
Just one innocent conversation away.
Friends talking about the past,
A word said, an image described,
Triggers a memory of a time, a place,
Someone, something to suppress.

You weren't thinking about it,
Not remotely on your mind.
A trigger pulled.
A memory recessed,
Shoots into your brain like a bullet.
Still has an impact to this day.

Raw, fervent emotions burst to the surface,
Like a volcano spewing unresolved hurts into the
atmosphere,
Your mind reloads, no longer present here,
Your mind shoots you back there!

Melissa, the Marathon Runner

Run Melissa -
Run because you can,
Run because it sparks a light within,
Run because it serves your heart,
As your heart serves others.
Heartfelt love runs the course.

My creation of Melissa Running

Run the course, Melissa!
We see the light in your heart!

Melissa, Marathon runner,
Run around, through and over,
Heart pounds cross the finish line!
See the light Melissa, the Light of the Heart!

Betty Eyes Her Future

Kind, sparkling, mischievous blue eyes,
Dim when she's hurting, sad, and cries,
Twinkle brightly with laughter,
Burn intensely with anger.

She's moving forward, on a new course,
Going to live her life, no remorse.
After all, she's Queen Mother and Jim's bride,
She's ready for the challenge, full of pride.

Don't forget her lucky "Penny,"
Not the copper kind of money.
Cute little rescue dog needed saving,
Found a Mama who knows she ain't misbehaving!

So, set sail on your cruising,
Say "buh bye" to all that bruising,
"Party hardy," enjoy boozing,
Girl you're a winner, you ain't loosing!

Obligation

A strange hold,
Squeezes, suffocates,
Sense of dread intensifies,
Heavy burden crushes
Duty constricts

Half-hearted,
Somewhat sincere
True intentions,
Or just obligations?

O   Oh
B   Boy
L   Listen
I   I'll
G   Get
A   At
T   That
I   In
O   Oh
N   Never

Re-define or Re-design?

Re-define or re-design; I <u>think</u> I'm fine?
Give up part of me, what is mine?
Look for some sort of special sign,
Stand by myself, alone, or intertwine?

We want our lives to shine,
Be bright, beautiful, benign,
Live on the edge of the sublime,
High on life from taste of the vine.

My pretty good life, why undermine,
Thought sends chills down my spine.
Maybe re-define and re-design,
Definite <u>no</u> to confine!

Medicine Chest

You are the medicine that soothes,
Using you like a drug,
Can't stop taking,
Doesn't get better,
Keeps needing more.

Won't overdose, too careful about that,
Just enough to soothe, dull the pain.
Seems to be getting better, looking hopeful,
Then regresses, back to status quo.

Clearly an addict, and you are the fix,
Using you as a panacea.
You don't realize it for a while.
Then, one day, you do.

You are their medicine chest.
They open you, admire what they see,
Take you off the shelf,
Take what they need from you.

Hold you in the palm of their hand,
Swallow you up.
Put you back, close the door.
Shut you out.
Shut you out of their life,

Until they need another fix,
Until they need <u>you</u> again,
To confide in, to confer with,
To soothe, to make <u>them</u> feel better.

It becomes a vicious cycle,
Needed, then discarded,
Over and again,
Used up, like an empty medicine bottle.
Used up, tossed in the trash bin.

When your medicine no longer soothes,
A new drug will be found to replace you,
Will take <u>your</u> place on the shelf.
The cycle continues,
A new fix to soothe the addiction.

Unravel

At what point does a life begin to unravel?
Does it start with a little tug?
Unconsciously, barely noticed,
Dismissed with a shrug?
How many tugs accompanied with shrugs?

Does it start with a string pulled?
Is it a tug of the heart string?
Is it a yank on your chain?
Have you become controlled by a string?
Are you someone's puppet on a string?
Controlled by an outer force?

Does it happen at birth when the cord is cut?
When life commences?
Does it happen later when forced into adulthood?
When parents cut the cord,
Finally, no strings attached.

Is that the end of unraveling?
When no strings left to pull?
Push and pull
Give and take

Ball of string, tightly wound up
Do we start out all wound up?

Over time unravel like a ball of yarn?
Do we chase after life?
Like the cat that chases the ball of yarn,
Always trying to grab hold of that loose string?

If we grab onto to the end of the string
Does that save us?
Is it like a life line?
What if we let go?

Are we strung along?
High strung.
Strung out
String up.
String someone along.

If you've been strung along
When do you realize it?
Is there a tug?
Or series of tugs?
Or just one huge tug?

Do you feel the tugs?
Do you sense them, but ignore them?
Are you aware but tuck the tugs away?
Do tiny tugs intensify?
How many and how intense?
Until a tiny tug is now a body slam!

Now waves of wake-up calls that beckoned you,
Knock you down.
Take notice, the coverings, the trappings of your life
Slowly, one by one,
Unravel in front of your eyes, and you barely see it.

Unbeknownst to you,
The tiny tugs dismissed, overlooked,
Ignored for years are now body slams,
Not to be ignored.

Knock down, Knock out,
Knock, Knock, are you still there,
Living what's left of your life?

The Pandora Bracelet

The gift was delivered in a small box one special
Christmas,
Two initials and one red charm,
An aquamarine later to celebrate my March madness,
I don't really see any harm.

Fuchsia hearts for love,
Pink ribbons for cancer,
Charms that never move,
Lovingly, I wear her.

I now possess a Pandora bracelet.
Am I buying into the unknown future,
Celebrating special times in life met
With icons representing the past captured?

In the end of days when I'm old,
I will so, so often wonder,
What stories will the bracelet hold?
Oh, to ponder, oh to ponder!

Chapter Four - *Perfectly Natural*

Mother Nature is a Terrorist
Must be on constant watch for her!
Disguises herself as man or woman,
Changes name to suit her temperament,
Never uses her "favorites" again.

She changed the course of history.
Permanently altered coastlines.
Made front page news.
Closed down Wall Street.

Strategically positions cells on map,
Relentless, organized, elusive,
Ever erupting, weather vane, volatile.
Formidable, fueled with enduring fury.

Targets where ever and whatever pleases her,
Strikes without warning, although tracked on radar,
Rains down utter destruction.
There is no escape.

Relies on strong formations,
Masses along ridges,
Columns of storm clouds.
Wages lightning war.
She makes dust swirl,
Clouds rotate, winds shear,
Glaciers melt, oceans overflow,
Earth shake.

She spews, chokes, poisons,
Hails, freezes, floods,
Scorches, parches, burns,
Causes death and despair.

She lurks in the Alley,
Lays siege to the Heartland,
Obliterates towns and lives,
Scars the earth in her path.

Uses rotation as weapon of mass destruction,
Thunder and lightning as scare tactics,
Causes outbreak of fear and panic.
Stuns with shock and awe.

She is amused when they try to fight back,
Digging their firewalls and filling their sandbags,
Hiding in their basements, and "hunkering down."
Those who chase and get too close, she exacts revenge!
Always plotting next strike,

Warnings issued,
Complacency settles in,
They let down their guard.

She waits.
She strikes.
There is no defense.
She takes no prisoners.

The Storm Dreader

It's late, it's storming,
Thunder, lightning,
Intermittent wind gusts,
Please just end, just end, just…

I will always be afraid.
Skies blacken, dark clouds invade.
Raindrops become pellets,
Assaulting like jets.

Too terrified to sleep,
Look out window, take a peep.
Pace through the house, look north, then west,
Steal a few glances, cannot rest.

At attention, like a sentinel,
Waiting for "all clear" signal.
All my senses on high alert,
Although my body feels inert.

What time is it? Has it passed?
How much longer can it last?
Want to close my eyes, have to sleep,
If I do, from bed I might leap!

Did I just hear the siren?
Wish the AC wasn't on
Did I imagine hearing it?
Why isn't that NOAA lit?
Loud sounds clashing,
Wind roars, rain slashing.
Sounds attack my equilibrium.
I listen, don't breathe, lose momentum.

Thank God the AC stopped running,
Only hear raindrops falling.
What time is it? Has it passed?

Stuck on the Weather Channel

Again, I am glued to the Weather Channel,
Like an annoying gnat stuck to fly paper.
Sucked in, inescapable,
Yellow glue so indestructible.

Clouds give rise,
Paper dries,
Both captives,
One dies, one lives.

Fate or curse?
Which death is worse?
A thousand deaths from weather worry,
Or a sticky kind in a hurry?

Finally, Sunshine!

Sunshine is the day's smile;
Greeting you with a fresh beginning.
Erasing yesterday.
Inspiring you to be your best.
Beckoning you to come out and play.
Calling you to lie in the grass, watch the cloud
formations float by.
Inviting you to 'sit awhile' on the porch.
Persuading you to find the perfect picnic spot.
Warming your skin.
Coaxing you to close your eyes and let your mind
wander.
Making you feel happy and carefree.
Thrilling you with new discoveries.
Luring you on an adventure.
Fortifying you with energy.
Whispering 'don't go in, stay a little longer, five more
minutes.
Encouraging you to linger.
Staying with you all day like a best friend.

Drawing to a close,
Promising to come back.
You'll recognize that smile again, anywhere!

Beauty Felled

Garnets, rubies, citrine,
Forest's crown jewels,
Boasting brilliance.
Beauty dazzles.

Softly surrendering,
Silently drifting,
Smothering.
Beauty fades.

Withered, weathered,
Wind-whipped,
Tossed, tumbled,
Beauty weeps.

Scattered sacrifices,
Last proof of life,
Imprints on sidewalk.
Leaves lament.

Crisp, crunchy.
Rakes eradicate,
Mowers mutilate.
We weep.

White Weather

I hate the way the wind blows,
Especially when driving snows
Scream sideways at bent-over trees
Bringing humanity to its knees.

I hate the way the wind howls,
Never phasing wide-eyed owls
As they perch high atop the chimneys
Watching so cautiously, you and me.

Beneath those wide watchful eyes,
We shovel under darkened skies.
One owl hoots, then the other,
Snow flakes swirl, softly smother.

They keep us company as we clear.
The pair at a distance, never near.
We are separate, but together,
Inhabitants sharing white weather.

Soft, Warm Water

Sometimes, I just like to let my skin breathe
After washing away the layers of the day.
Most times, pampering with velvety creams,
Occasionally, covering only with air.

Makeup becomes a mask to hide behind,
Stripping it away at the end of the day,
Reveals the true essence of my being,
A soul, a spirit that needs healing.

Clean skin, a pureness penetrates,
Physical, Spiritual bodies renew.
Soft water, and a warm sunshine caress.
My Spirit soars to the stars.

I want to roam in the woodlands,
Savor the taste of sweet wine,
Give thanks for life under the stars,
Hope for a born-again life.

I want to outsmart the boogey man,
Fly with the tooth fairy,
Find my wild child,
Discover who I am <u>now.</u>

I want the spirit, grace and magic
That is the "Goddess of Lynn,"
Be a bright beacon of light,
Draw me back to soft, warm, healing water.

Je Suis un Artiste

Always thought of myself as creative,
Though through the years left brain I did live.

Now I am indulging in art classes,
Not the kind that attract the masses,
Painting at Peabody Estate,
Cantigny, McCormick of late.

To my astonishment, I have talent,
It's been undeveloped, even latent.
Just learning, experimenting with colors,
Interest, curiosity open doors.

My thoughts, words give birth to life as art,
Unwritten journey, baby step start.
Composition, colors compose the story,
The Arts collide in my mind's eye in glory.

My imagination soars, lifting the veil of mist.
Beckoning me to be both author and artist.

My Mosaic Masterpiece

A glorious day in my exploration of the arts!
Learned about heels and shards,
Mortar spreads like butter,
Plates split in half with one snip.

Shards of varying shapes and colors,
Create a puzzle, then un-puzzle,
Re-creating the pattern imagined,
Working against mortar's short life span.

If not careful, might end up a sticky mess,
Feels like beat the clock, I confess.
Voila` I created my first piece,
Stepping stone of roses and pearls.

Its home is waiting in my rose jardin,
My first attempt at this ancient art,
Honestly, I am quite pleased.
Magnifique!

Windows

Windows bear witness to passage of time.
Windows serve dual purposes,
You can look out, you can look in.
They start the day, end the day.

Raise the shades, morning light,
Take a moment, stand there, look out,
Graced by the beams so bright,
Lower the shades, sleepy night,
End the day with a good night.
New day, now done day!

Old windows, new windows.
Weep from droplets of rain,
Allow people to peer inside,
Seek their own reflection,
Birds crash at their attraction.

Twinkle with evening stars so old,
Barricade us against the cold,
Ward off westerly winds,
Reflect electric javelins,
Glisten with frozen snow,
Warn of swirling storms.

Warm from sun's rays,
Keep darkness at bay,
Sweat with fog and dew,
Greet the morning anew,
Usher in soft, cool breezes,
Ice over when condensation freezes,
Replace, never, well maybe, it can be a pane!

Dream Catcher

Which dreams are caught,
An ancient craft taught,
So long ago in distant time,
Now, silent as today's mime?

Are caught dreams prisoners,
With untold stories, no futures,
Yearning to escape to the great beyond,
Dancing like fireflies on moonlit pond?

Which dreams escape, which dreams are kept,
What if dream already dreamt,
Or slips away through a crack,
What if it's darker than black?

What Entity, what Being
Has the power deciding
With revered and fabled ability,
Decisions made hastily or sensibly?

A dream's fate or future
Drifts into the dream catcher,
Snags like an insect in a spider's web,
Or gently floats out to sea on tide's ebb.

Reflections in a Gazing Ball

Reflections seen:
Absolute truths
Singular hopes
Secret dreams
Curious eyes

Too truthful to bear.
Centered or off-balance.
Luminous like the super moon.
Radiant like the noon sun.

Senses awakened:
Well being
Serenity
Acceptance
Uncertainty

Always dwelling within,
Sometimes buried, sometimes forgotten.
Always desiring endless attention,
Sometimes met with apprehension.

Concentration channels clarity.
Contemplation illuminates.
Meditation soothes, calms.
Reflection creates passageways.

The Thing About Crystal Balls

Sometimes you feel you just have to know the outcome,
There must be some measure of certainty,
Someway to minimize the risk,
Someway to protect.

If I could be certain I wouldn't get hurt again,
Some measure of reassurance,
A green light that says "go,"
A way to take the worry out of living.

If I could be certain they wouldn't leave me.
If I could be certain they were the "right one."

If I had a crystal ball
That could show me my future,
How present would I be today?
How hard would I work for tomorrow?

Would you take a relationship for granted?
Because you knew for certain,
They would always be there.

Would you stop trying so hard,
Become less of a partner,
Less of a lover?

What if you gazed inside?

94

And saw an entirely different scenario?
One which has <u>you</u> leaving the relationship?
And you were worried about him leaving you!
The thing about a crystal ball,

It can see from <u>both </u>sides,
Foretell the expected,
Frighten with unexpected.

Shatter the crystal ball,
Crystalized certainties climb to the sky
Clouds, winds, whirl them upward,

Find refuge in the vastness,
Find home in heaven,
From whence they came.

The Spark! To Sparkle!

I attended a two-person play, <u>Botanic Garden</u>, recently on a Sunday evening. As the married couple in the play were arguing, the word "spark" was used, more like a weapon than a noun. So strongly and repeatedly the word was used, it got me thinking about what "spark" is and the many interpretations of "spark". In the play the husband accuses the wife of losing her "spark", and in doing so, has ruined their marriage.

Do we each have a "spark?" Can we "sparkle" some of the time, and not at all other times? In some, it shines so brightly other people can see it a mile away. Yet in others, not even sure they have the faintest ember. I believe that "Spark" is our essence. It's a raging wildfire burning out of control in the gut, deep within our cellular structure and makes us feel alive, feel on fire! Feel like we are burning up! It's the fuel that stokes our thoughts, our creativity, our interaction and response to the people, space, time, and natural wonder that comprises the continuum that envelops us.

It's this energy that ignites and creates a spark
It's this spark that creates the light within us that others see
It's this spark in their eyes that you see that says "they get it"

It's this spark in their eyes that you see that says "they get me"

It's this spark that makes us ever so witty
It's this smirk because you're the only one who gets it
It's this playfulness, "you're fun"
It's this still a wild child inside, you know it, but they don't
It's this Mona Lisa smile when you think you've pulled it off
It's this thrill when you win, yes women like to win
It's this glint in your eye when someone's flirting with you
It's this glint in your eye when you realize you've been flirting back
It's this chemical attraction just waiting to combust
It's this attraction you don't understand and can't explain
It's this sexy, sensuous, beautiful wild woman
It's this "yeah baby"

It's this sweetheart
It's this unstoppable chain reaction
It's what "gives you fever"
It's what makes your heart beat wildly inside your chest
It's what makes you sweat
It's this urge that needs to create and see art
It's this awareness of beauty

It's this capacity to see purpose
It's this excitement in giving new life to something old
or used
It's this gratitude after helping, giving back or
volunteering
It's this joy in making someone happy
It's loving the life you have imagined
It's loving the life you have created
It's loving yourself
It's loving that one special person
It's loving your family
It's loving your friends
It's being in love

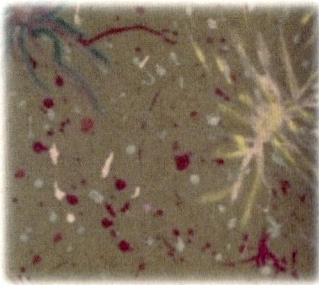

The Path

I still don't see my path.
It hasn't been disclosed to me.
I don't know how to find it.
I look, read, I'm open, aware
Will it lead me where I think I want to go?
Will it take me in an entirely different direction?
Will it be a super highway?
Slow winding country road,
Tree covered forest trail,
Narrow, single footpath.
Will there be signs or markers to show me the way?
Or will I have to find my way on my own?
I still don't see my path.
Walking alone, or with company?

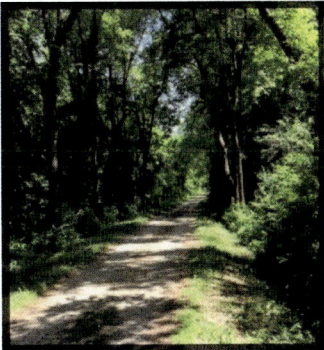

Familiar Roads

These are familiar roads,
Roads that I know,
Roads that take me where I need to go
Take me there fast, take me there slow,
There's no in-between, just go!

These are familiar roads,
Roads that we traveled,
In good times and bad times,
Taking us to happy places.

These are familiar roads,
Roads that we've been down before,
Roads that twist and turn,
Be cautious, danger ahead,
Road kill on the shoulder.

My Mother's Eyes

When I look at myself in the mirror,
I see my Mother's brown eyes staring back,
Knowing Death would be her last visitor.
I close my eyes, sad, my emotions crack.

I want to remember eyes with expression,
Not lifeless eyes devoid of sensory.
I offer no plausible explanation,
This sight forever haunts my memory.

In my eyes, our brown eyes are one.
She is dead but lives in my mirror.
I long to see her, but Death won.
Each morning two pair of eyes appear.

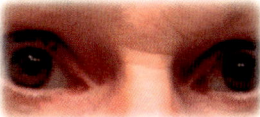

The Ties That Bind

Two lives bound together,
Marriage knot tied securely,
Never to come loose.
One to the other, a loving tether.

The ties' hues blend with each other,
As do these two colorful personalities.
With each other, created a colorful palette,
Painting a picture of a life envisioned,
Weaving together two lives and families.

Life's design is full of colors and experiences,
Rich and deep.
A tie's design is full of colors and textures.
Bold and traditional.
Both come together in a cohesive pattern.

Ties tell the story of the wearer;
Where he's been,
Where he's going,
His favorite color,
His playful side,
His conviction,
People in his life,
His scent.

The fabric of their lives,
Intricately woven together,
Like the ties on the pillow.
Small pieces of your beloved,
His scent still lingering on the fabric,
To hold close to your heart,
To hold in your arms and hug,
To rest your head on and remember,
To comfort you and cushion your loss.

Chapter Five - *Fragmented Feelings*

Impermanence

You appeared out of nowhere.
There, just one night.
Probing conversation,
Flirting.

You went away.
Stayed in my head.
Dimming memory,
Adjusting.

You appeared out of nowhere, again.
Here to stay awhile.
Lingering this time,
Hugging.

Time, space, two souls entangle.
Cosmic blink of an eye.
For a second, we are us, now just you and me.
Universal impermanence!

Someday, can we walk once again in the footprints left
behind?
Someday, can we break the dam holding back emotions

Someday, can river of emotions flow smoothly over
jagged edges
Left behind by other lovers' good intentions?

In a blink, the universe opens up,
Two souls searching for existence of love.
One finds tenderness, perspective, and ability to love
again.
One finds warmth, tenderness and possibility to love
again.
Both love … impermanence.

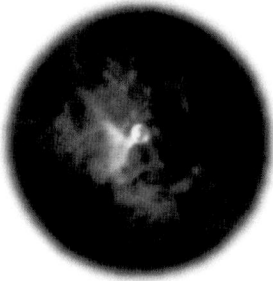

Will I Ever See Him Again?

What is it like to remember cried tears,
Raw, aching emotions, feelings and fears
From the last, long and lonely twenty years?

Minutes and hours at first, not breathing,
Days and weeks, not sleeping, not eating.
Months become years, never forgetting.

Through the years, there were four sightings; tokens,
Neither stopped, never any words spoken,
Too empty, too scared, too proud, too broken.

Wonder how he looks, how altered?
What words would softly be uttered?
Any explanation offered?

I'd like to see him.
Talk
Listen
Touch
Maybe embrace
Maybe kiss
Maybe NOT!

New Life

When you start a new life,
You hope it exceeds the old.
You hope you find happiness.
You hope you can find comfort,
Among strangers' feigned interest.

When you start a new life,
Escaping from and running to,
Does not guarantee happiness.

There really is no such thing as a "new" life,
You can't escape from yourself,
You can't run away from yourself.

It is still you, only transplanted elsewhere.
Your "new" life carries reality of "old" life,
This luggage of reality travels with you,
This luggage circles on the carousel!

Count Every Day

Every day, every beautiful day without you
Is a loss and is lost; lost to time's end.
Never to re-imagine, re-call, re-live.
Every day that is lost to us;
We did not walk together, we did not hug,
We did not feel breezes whispering on our skin,
We did not feel sun warming our faces,
We did not share smiles, glances with each other,
Meanings only known to us.

How many days, how many countless days
Do you think you possess?
How many days can you afford to be away?
How many days can you fritter away?
How many days you can throw away?
Our time and our days are not endless.
Every day is numbered,
We are only granted so many.
They will run out. When exactly? We don't know.

Can you afford to spend any day without affection, attachment?

Without a shining light to help you find your way even on dark days?
Days meant to share with another,
Not recklessly thrown away, fearful to face the day.
Welcome every day.
Be thankful for every day.
Count every bright day and every dark day.
Count them all until time's end.
Until time's end, make them all count.

Plight

It's too bad you don't see the light,
You only see your own plight.
You don't realize how tired I am of the fight,
It's too bad you don't see me in the light.

I must tell you, very leery, but it's right.
I'm just so weary, tell with paper, pen and write.

Don't Gotta

Don't gotta leave!
She said with sigh, heave.
Don't gotta go!
She cares so.

Don't gotta hide.
You have pride.
Don't gotta run.
Stay have fun.

Don't gotta start anew,
Right here, will do.

Gotta leave, gotta leave,
He said with sigh, heave.

Gotta go.
Feel so, so.
Gotta ride.
Sorta lied.

Gotta run.
Was fun.
Start anew.
Bid her adieu.

I'm Sorry

I'm sorry.
Don't know what happened,
Walls let down,
Now, all known.

I'm sorry,
Didn't want to come to this,
Not enough room,
Too much gloom.

I'm sorry.
Didn't want to hurt you,
Need to be free,
Too much for me.

I'm sorry.
Don't want to end friendship,
It can be,
Don't you see?

In the Midst

How can a person be lonely
In the midst of so many?
A smile, a nod,
A look in the eyes,
A short conversation.
Yet sadly,
No real connection.

We know each other's names,
But not the person,
Who they are,
What they think,
What is their life story?

Where are the ones,
Who really know us,
Who really love us,
Close at hand or far away.
Life-long friend or new?

How many people do we let in?
Open our hearts to,
Trust with our deepest secrets and thoughts?
Maybe one person, half way.
Half way scares me!

Tonight, It Seems

Everyone around me is part of a relationship,
I am not and have not been for a long time.
I feel cheated,
I feel I am missing out,
Not special to someone,
Always the one without someone,
Just me, by myself, here with everyone else.

How did my life end up like this?
What did I do to deserve this?
Where did I go wrong?
When did my path become unrecognizable to me?

I don't see or understand my path,
I don't know how to find it,
I don't think it's been shown to me yet.
Maybe it has, and I stumbled over it.
Maybe it has, and I went the wrong way.
Maybe it has, and I didn't recognize it.

Should I be looking for someone?
Someone who is on my path?
Someone with whom I'll share my path?
Someone who will walk by my side?

About the Author

Lynn Martin McHale is 68 years old, grew up in Middletown, New Jersey and resides in the suburbs of Chicago, IL She retired from Sears in 2012 after 41 years working in various positions in the store and corporate office. She has one son, who is married, and has two beautiful, little grandsons.

She lives in a retirement community and is very active; Parkinson's Support Group Leader, Chairman of The Treasure Chest, Swim Class Instructor, Sales Ambassador, Travel Committee. Lynn was involved in the APDA (American Parkinson's Disease Association) Midwest Chapter for 4 year as board member, Treasurer, and President of Board.

In 2005 Lynn was diagnosed with stage 2 breast cancer, which she fought with chemotherapy, lumpectomy, some nodes removed and radiation. It has been 13 years and still cancer free – a survivor. When she turned 60, the night of her birthday celebration she came down with shingles, the most painful thing she has ever experienced. Once again, a survivor!

Then a few months later she noticed a change in her gait, she was tipping forward, she couldn't write very well. It was very small and unreadable. She looked up symptoms, and by now you know the answer. Yes, she was diagnosed with Parkinson's disease!
Lynn was absolutely devastated. She took the diagnosis as a death sentence. She thought she had already fought and won her biggest battle; breast cancer. Now Parkinson's!!!???

Lynn has been writing on and off during her life at times of crisis, loss, heart break, disappointment or when she needed to make a monumental decision. She has notebooks tucked away in drawers. When she was diagnosed with Parkinson's disease, she was devastated and did not know what to do, where to go, whom to turn to, or what was her next step. She was frightened, could not see her future, did not know how to cope and spent a lot of time catastrophizing.

Lynn's quest for finding a way to cope, accept and manage her diagnosis led her support group, exercise and art therapy classes, and to seek help with a neuro-psychologist. So new crisis, and out came a new notebook. The words poured out onto the pages in poetic style. She discovered writing was therapeutic. It helped ease the anger, desperation and hopelessness she felt. Her writing became the poetry and voice of her soul. She started writing about PD, then transitioned to what inspires her, what she observes, how she feels, what she experiences in her life.

Over time, she found her way through her Parkinson's diagnosis; had a few "tune-ups" as she called them with neuro-psychologist and found what to do, where to go, whom to turn to and her path filled with all her next steps. She now laughs and says she has taken thousands of steps. After time, she started writing about what inspired her; maybe a word or phrase, something heard, or something seen, or something that moved her emotionally or she experienced. Inspiration can come from just about anything.

A little over a year after diagnosis, she retired and started taking art classes and art therapy for people with Parkinson's. The art therapy instructor was wonderful, talented and compassionate. This opened up a whole new world to her. Her favorite art is creating botanical print wreaths and leaves. She also loves to work with watercolor paint and pencil. Lynn discovered she really enjoyed painting and creating, and was actually pretty good, to her surprise! She says it transports her to another place, a place where your PD symptoms are set aside, and she gets lost in the experience of creation. So, she continues the creative process by painting, writing and photography. She calls it "indulging herself in the arts" and living with Parkinson's.

Lynn's debut book of poetry, photographs and photos of original art is the expression of her journey through the darkness of her diagnosis to the place of light and acceptance. She hopes some of the poems, or a few phrases or words comfort and encourage you, even inspire you.

"Oak Hydrangea"
Lynn McHale

121

62399451R00075

Made in the USA
Middletown, DE
25 August 2019